Animals and the Environment

by Jennifer Boothroyd

first step non-fiction

Lerner Books • London • New York • Minneapolis

Animals need
the **environment.**

Animals use land and water.

Snakes hide under rocks.

Some animals live under the ground.

Fish live in water.

Animals drink water.

Animals use other animals
and plants.

Owls eat small **rodents.**

Monkeys clean each other.

Cows eat grass.

Rabbits hide in the grass.

Animals **adapt** to their environment.

Giraffes have long necks to reach leaves in tall trees.

14

Lions have **sharp** teeth
to eat meat.

Birds fly to warmer places
in the winter.

Animals use the environment in many ways.

The Red Kite Returns

A red kite is a bird of prey with a forked tail and deep red feathers. Hundreds of years ago there were lots of red kites. People began killing them. They thought that they were a threat to farming. Kites nearly became extinct in the UK. In the early 1900s people began reintroducing and protecting red kites. Today, the red kite population is successfully increasing across the UK.

Animal Facts

 Scientists have discovered over one million different plants and animals. Most scientists believe there are millions that haven't been discovered yet.

 Many animals have become extinct in the last hundred years. Extinct means those animals have died out. None of those animals are left in the world.

 Thousands of birds, animals and fish around the world are endangered. Endangered means the animal is likely to become extinct.

 Some animals are helpful to humans. A brown bat can eat 600 mosquitoes in one hour.

 Some animals cause problems for humans. Rabbits can damage farmers' crops, reducing the harvest.

Glossary

 adapt – change

 environment – the land, water, air, weather and living things of the Earth

 sharp – able to cut or tear

 rodents – animals, such as mice and rats, that have large front teeth for gnawing

Index

adapt – 13

eat – 9, 11, 15, 21

hide – 4, 12

live – 5, 6

plants – 8, 11, 14, 20

water – 3, 6, 7

Rosewarne
Learning Centre

The images in this book are used with the permission of: © John R Kreul/Independent Picture Service, pp 2, 22 (second from top); PhotoDisc Royalty Free by Getty Images, pp 3, 5, 6, 7, 8, 13, 14, 17, 22 (top); © Joe McDonald/Visuals Unlimited, p 4; © Michael Quinton, pp 9, 22 (bottom); © Jonathan & Angela/Taxi/Getty Images, p 10; Agricultural Research Service, USDA, p 11; © Leonard Lee Rue III, p 12; © Royalty-Free/CORBIS, pp 15, 22 (second from bottom); © David W Hamilton/The Image Bank/Getty Images, p 16; Istockphoto.com/Christoph Achenbach, p 18.

Front cover: Royalty-Free/Corbis

First published in the United Kingdom in 2009 by
Lerner Books,
Dalton House,
60 Windsor Avenue,
London SW19 2RR

Website address: www.lernerbooks.co.uk

This edition was edited and updated for UK publication by Discovery Books Ltd.,
Unit 3, 37 Watling Street, Leintwardine, Shropshire, SY7 0LW

British Library Cataloguing in Publication Data

Boothroyd, Jennifer, 1972-
  Animals and the environment. - (First step nonfiction. Ecology)
  1. Animal ecology - Juvenile literature 2. Animals - Juvenile literature
  I. Title
  591.7

  ISBN-13: 978 0 7613 4302 8

Text copyright © 2008 by Lerner Publishing Group, Inc.

First published in the United States of America in 2008
Printed in Singapore